ELEMENTS OF **LIFE**

OXYGEN

NANCY DICKMANN

PowerKiDS press.

Published in 2019 by **The Rosen Publishing Group, Inc.**
29 East 21st Street, New York, NY 10010

Cataloging-in-Publication Data
Names: Dickmann, Nancy.
Title: Oxygen / Nancy Dickmann.
Description: New York : PowerKids Press, 2019. | Series: Elements of life | Includes glossary and index.
Identifiers: ISBN 9781538347652 (pbk.) | ISBN 9781538347676 (library bound) | ISBN 9781538347669 (6pack)
Subjects: LCSH: Oxygen--Juvenile literature. | Gases--Juvenile literature. | Chemical elements--Juvenile literature.
Classification: LCC QD181.O1 D53 2019 | DDC 546'.721--dc23

For Brown Bear Books Ltd:
Text and Editor: Nancy Dickmann
Designer and Illustrator: Supriya Sahai
Design Manager: Keith Davis
Picture Manager: Sophie Mortimer
Editorial Director: Lindsey Lowe
Children's Publisher: Anne O'Daly

Concept development: Square and Circus/Brown Bear Books Ltd

Picture Credits
Front Cover: Artwork, Supriya Sahai.
Interior: iStock: 3DSculptor, 25t, Berkut, 25b, daviles, 24, Steve Debenport, 16, gianniNYK, 6–7, Neil Lockhart, 21t, MartinM303, 5, mikeuk, 19, MrPants, 12, scanrail, 7, SolStock, 17, somchaij, 23b; NASA: Earth Observatory, 21b; Shutterstock: decade3d-anatomy online, 15, 29t, expert, 14, JGade, 23tl, Matva, 22, 29b, oksmit, 8, Horst Ulbrich, 9, 28.
Key: t=top, b=bottom, c=center, l=left, r=right

Brown Bear Books have made every attempt to contact the copyright holders. If you have any information please contact licensing@brownbearbooks.co.uk

Manufactured in the United States of America

CPSIA Compliance Information: Batch CWPK19: For Further Information contact Rosen Publishing, New York, New York at 1-800-237-9932

CONTENTS

ELEMENTS ALL AROUND US

Everything in the universe is made up of elements. These substances cannot be broken down into other substances. Living things are made mainly from six elements. They are oxygen, carbon, hydrogen, nitrogen, phosphorus, and sulfur.

ATOMS AND MOLECULES

Elements are made up of atoms. These tiny particles are much too small to see. They are made up of even smaller particles called protons, neutrons, and electrons. The protons and neutrons are in the nucleus in the center of the atom. Atoms can exist on their own. They can also join up with atoms of another element to form a compound. A compound might look and behave very differently from the original elements.

Electrons

Neutrons

Protons

THE OXYGEN ATOM

An oxygen atom has 8 electrons and 8 protons. Most have 8 neutrons, but a few have 9 or 10.

OXYGEN EVERYWHERE

You can find oxygen anywhere on Earth. It is in the air that we breathe and the ground that we stand on. The water that fills rivers, lakes, and oceans is made of oxygen combined with hydrogen. It is in the bodies of all living things!

Oxygen and hydrogen are both gases. They join together to form water, which is a liquid.

Natural or Not?

There are about 94 elements that are found in nature. Others have been made in laboratories.

PHYSICAL PROPERTIES OF OXYGEN

Every element has characteristics called physical properties. They can be observed or measured without changing the element into another substance.

DIFFERENT FORMS

Most oxygen in the air is made of molecules with two oxygen atoms. There is another form of oxygen, called ozone. This has molecules made up of three oxygen atoms. These different forms of the same element are called allotropes. They have different properties.

Oxygen dissolves in water. Ocean plants and animals depend on this oxygen.

LOOKING AT OXYGEN

Even though we can't see or touch pure oxygen, we can use our senses to observe some of its physical properties. An element's color and odor are physical properties. The temperature at which it condenses is a physical property, too.

STATE: Oxygen is a gas at room temperature.

At very low temperatures, oxygen becomes a liquid. It is stored in special tanks.

COLOR: Oxygen is transparent, meaning see-through. Ozone is also a gas at room temperature, but it has a bluish color.

ODOR: Oxygen has no odor. Some people describe ozone's odor as being like chlorine, or the "clean" smell of rain.

CONDUCTIVITY: Oxygen is a poor conductor of heat and electricity.

CHEMICAL PROPERTIES OF OXYGEN

Oxygen is one of the most reactive of all the elements. It reacts with most elements to form compounds. Oxygen also reacts with lots of compounds. It pushes other elements out of a compound. It takes their place to make a new compound.

CHEMICAL CHANGES

When an element combines with another, a chemical change takes place. The atoms have been reordered into new arrangements. The element's chemical properties can be observed when this happens. These include how readily it forms bonds, and how easily it burns.

The limestone in these cliffs is a compound that contains oxygen, carbon, and calcium.

When iron reacts with water and oxygen, it forms a compound called iron oxide, more commonly known as rust.

ALL ABOUT OXYGEN

Here are a few of oxygen's chemical properties:

Oxygen itself does not burn, but it helps other substances burn.

Oxygen reacts with carbon to form carbon dioxide (CO_2) or carbon monoxide (CO).

Oxygen often "steals" electrons from other atoms and compounds in a process called oxidation.

Compounds of an element with oxygen are called oxides.

PHYSICAL OR CHEMICAL?

A physical change, such as water freezing into ice, is easy to reverse. When the temperature rises, the ice will melt back into water. But when two or more elements react, they form a completely different substance. A chemical change is much harder to reverse.

WHERE IS OXYGEN FOUND?

Oxygen is all around you! In some places, such as the air, it exists in its pure form. There is also a lot of oxygen locked up in different compounds.

HOW OXYGEN WAS DISCOVERED

In the 1400s, Italian artist Leonardo da Vinci suggested that air was made up of at least two gases. About 300 years later, two chemists discovered oxygen. Carl Scheele in Sweden and Joseph Priestley in England were working separately but got the same results. A French chemist called Antoine Lavoisier soon found that when substances burn, they are combining with oxygen in the air.

Humans and animals breathe out carbon dioxide, a gas made of carbon and oxygen. It forms part of the atmosphere.

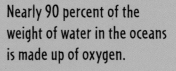

Nearly 90 percent of the weight of water in the oceans is made up of oxygen.

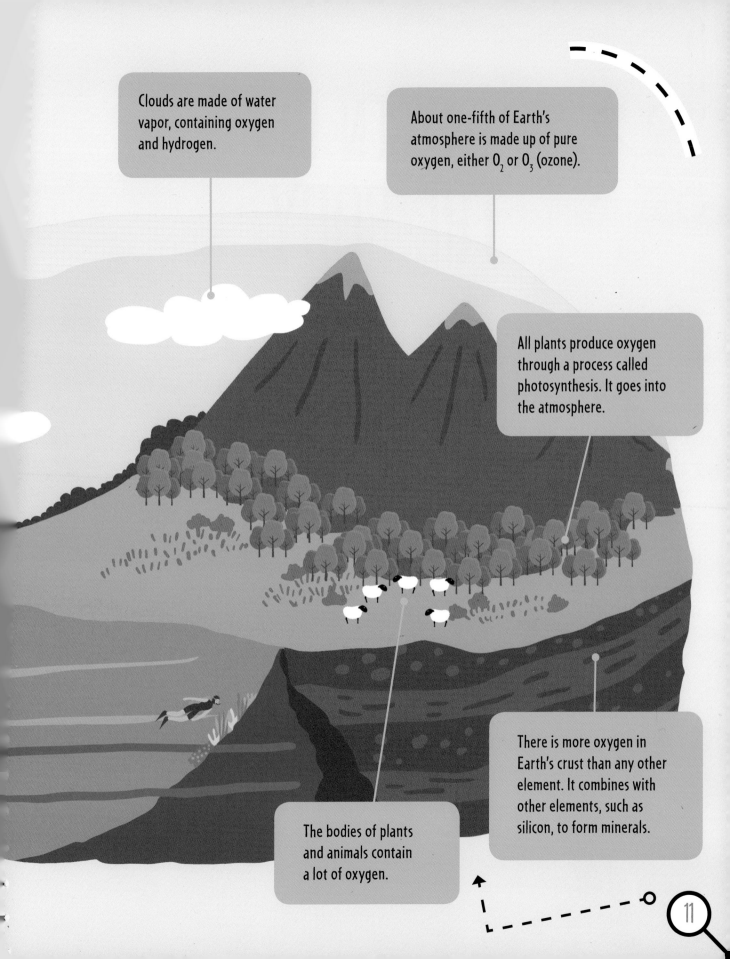

Clouds are made of water vapor, containing oxygen and hydrogen.

About one-fifth of Earth's atmosphere is made up of pure oxygen, either O_2 or O_3 (ozone).

All plants produce oxygen through a process called photosynthesis. It goes into the atmosphere.

There is more oxygen in Earth's crust than any other element. It combines with other elements, such as silicon, to form minerals.

The bodies of plants and animals contain a lot of oxygen.

OXYGEN IN THE BODY

Your body is made up of trillions of tiny cells. Each one contains some oxygen. With every breath, you take in more oxygen.

THE BIG FOUR

About 96 percent of the human body is made up of just four elements: oxygen, carbon, hydrogen, and nitrogen. Oxygen alone makes up 65 percent of your body's mass. There are actually more atoms of hydrogen in the body than any other element. But oxygen atoms are heavier, so they make up a larger proportion of the overall mass.

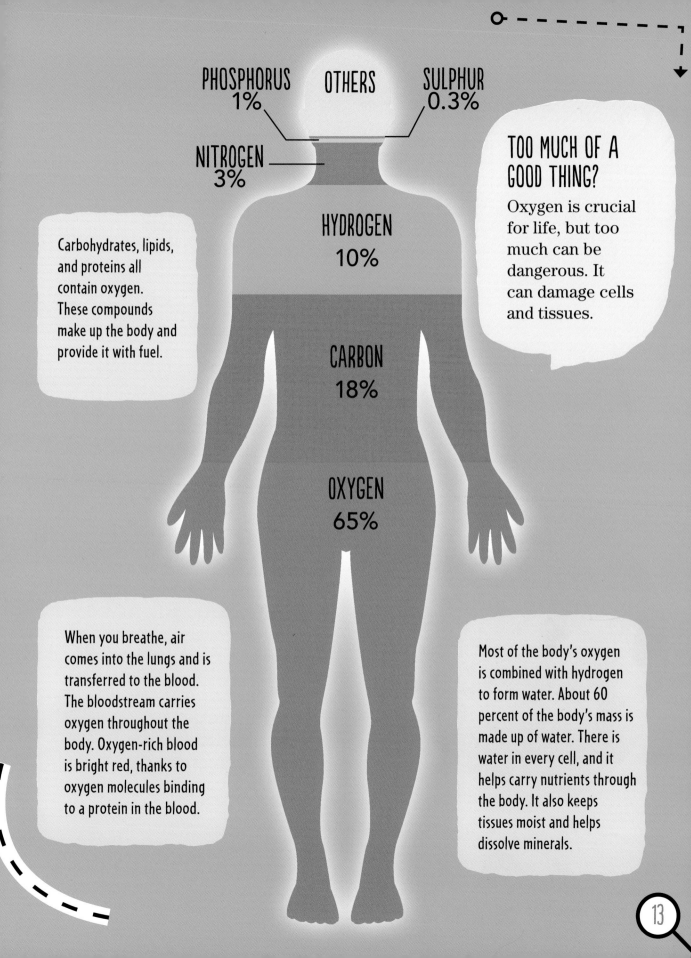

PHOSPHORUS
1%

OTHERS

SULPHUR
0.3%

NITROGEN
3%

HYDROGEN
10%

CARBON
18%

OXYGEN
65%

Carbohydrates, lipids, and proteins all contain oxygen. These compounds make up the body and provide it with fuel.

TOO MUCH OF A GOOD THING?

Oxygen is crucial for life, but too much can be dangerous. It can damage cells and tissues.

When you breathe, air comes into the lungs and is transferred to the blood. The bloodstream carries oxygen throughout the body. Oxygen-rich blood is bright red, thanks to oxygen molecules binding to a protein in the blood.

Most of the body's oxygen is combined with hydrogen to form water. About 60 percent of the body's mass is made up of water. There is water in every cell, and it helps carry nutrients through the body. It also keeps tissues moist and helps dissolve minerals.

LIFE ON EARTH

Earth is the only planet in the solar system with an oxygen-rich atmosphere. We take our oxygen for granted, but it hasn't always been there.

WHERE DID IT COME FROM?

When the planet first formed, most oxygen quickly formed compounds in the crust. Early life-forms didn't need oxygen. But eventually a type of organism called cyanobacteria appeared. These tiny living things produce oxygen. By about 2.4 billion years ago, they had produced enough oxygen to collect in the atmosphere. This made all other forms of life possible.

Other planets in our solar system have an atmosphere, including Venus and Mars. Only Earth's atmosphere supports life.

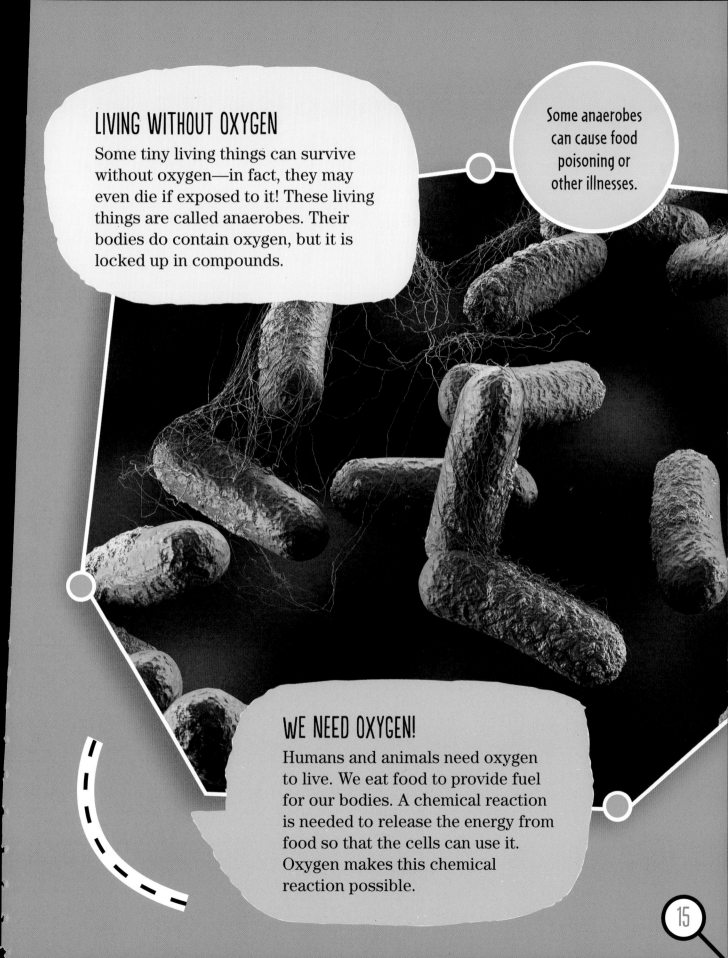

LIVING WITHOUT OXYGEN

Some tiny living things can survive without oxygen—in fact, they may even die if exposed to it! These living things are called anaerobes. Their bodies do contain oxygen, but it is locked up in compounds.

Some anaerobes can cause food poisoning or other illnesses.

WE NEED OXYGEN!

Humans and animals need oxygen to live. We eat food to provide fuel for our bodies. A chemical reaction is needed to release the energy from food so that the cells can use it. Oxygen makes this chemical reaction possible.

BREATHE IN, BREATHE OUT

How does oxygen get from the air into our cells?
What does it do once it's there? The answer is respiration!

HOW IT WORKS

After oxygen enters the lungs, it moves into the blood and is carried to the cells. Blood also carries a sugar called glucose to the cells. Inside each cell are tiny organs called mitochondria. Inside these mitochondria, a chemical reaction takes place. The glucose and oxygen combine to form water and carbon dioxide gas, while releasing energy.

The carbon dioxide produced in respiration is a waste product. It travels back to the lungs, and we breathe it out.

WHAT'S IN A NAME?

Some people use "respiration" to mean the act of breathing in and out. But breathing is a physical process, where muscles work to draw air in and out of the lungs. Respiration is a chemical process. It involves breaking down substances to release energy.

Exercise makes you breathe faster. The harder your body is working, the more oxygen you need.

Write It Down!

Chemical reactions can be written down as equations. The equation for respiration is:

glucose + oxygen → carbon dioxide + water (+ energy)

Energy is released in this reaction. It is written in parentheses because it is not a substance.

THE OXYGEN CYCLE

The oxygen we breathe today is the same oxygen that existed when dinosaurs roamed the earth. Oxygen atoms are constantly recycled in a process called the oxygen cycle.

1. In photosynthesis, plants produce oxygen, which goes into the air.

A PERFECT BALANCE

The amount of oxygen given off by plants is balanced by the amount of oxygen that animals take in. This means that the percentage of oxygen in the atmosphere stays constant at 21 percent.

4. Plants take in carbon dioxide, which they need for photosynthesis. Then the process repeats!

OTHER PATHWAYS

Not all oxygen atoms follow this simple process. Some oxygen in the air reacts with substances on the ground. For example, oxygen reacts with an iron roof to form rust, or an animal's oxygen-containing dead body breaks down into soil. Oxygen that is locked in compounds on the ground can sometimes be released back into the atmosphere. This process is called chemical weathering.

2. Animals take in the oxygen when they breathe.

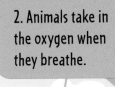

3. In respiration, animals' bodies use the oxygen and produce carbon dioxide. They breathe out carbon dioxide.

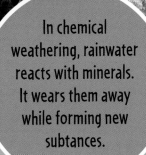

In chemical weathering, rainwater reacts with minerals. It wears them away while forming new subtances.

IN TWOS AND THREES

Even though oxygen and ozone are both made up of pure oxygen, they have different properties. However, we depend on them both!

ALL ABOUT OZONE

Ozone forms naturally high up in the atmosphere. Rays from the sun hit oxygen molecules (1), splitting them into two separate oxygen atoms (2). Each of these atoms can combine with a two-atom oxygen molecule, making a three-atom molecule of ozone (3).

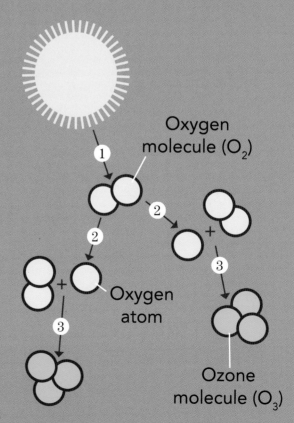

Oxygen molecule (O_2)

Oxygen atom

Ozone molecule (O_3)

Where is ozone found?

A lot of Earth's ozone is found high in the atmosphere. You can often smell ozone just before it rains, because the thunderstorm's winds push ozone down to the surface. Ozone can be formed by passing an electric spark through oxygen, so you can smell it near electrical machinery.

Ozone gets its name from the Greek word *ozein*, meaning "to smell."

THE OZONE LAYER

The ozone in the atmosphere forms a layer that blocks some types of harmful radiation from the sun. But scientists discovered that humans were causing a hole in the ozone layer. Chemicals, including some in spray cans, were turning ozone into oxygen. International agreements banned some of the chemicals that reduced ozone levels, and levels are slowly going back up.

Dark blue and purple areas show the hole in the ozone layer over Antarctica.

1979

2011

OXYGEN AND BURNING

Burning is a chemical reaction, and it can't happen without oxygen. Another name for burning is combustion. It happens when a fuel reacts with oxygen.

The heat produced when wood burns is enough to toast marshmallows.

HOW IT WORKS

Fuels such as wood and coal contain compounds called hydrocarbons. Hydrocarbons react with oxygen to produce carbon dioxide and water. The reaction gives off heat and light, in the form of a flame.

BURNING OUT

If you cover a lighted candle with a glass, after a few seconds the flame will go out. This is because the combustion reaction has used up all the oxygen under the glass. When there is no more oxygen, the reaction stops.

OTHER REACTIONS

Combustion is a type of reaction called an oxidation reaction. Oxidation means adding oxygen. A sliced apple turning brown is also an oxidation reaction. Compounds in the apple react with oxygen in the air to make the brown color. Iron reacts with oxygen to make rust in another oxidation reaction.

To keep steel bridges from rusting, they are coated in paint. The paint keeps oxygen from coming into contact with the steel.

USING OXYGEN

Oxygen is vital for life, but it is useful in other ways, too. We use oxygen and oxygen products in our everyday lives.

Divers carry tanks of oxygen and other gases so they can breathe underwater. Some mountain climbers use oxygen tanks at high altitudes, where the air is thin.

To condense into a liquid, oxygen must be very cold. Liquid oxygen is used as a coolant in some rocket systems, and also for high-powered computers.

Rocket engines use liquid oxygen. It acts as an oxidizer, making the rocket fuel burn at an increased rate.

Airplane and submarine crews carry oxygen supplies in case of emergency.

Oxygen is used in the manufacturing of chemicals such as nitric acid and hydrogen peroxide.

In steelmaking, pure oxygen is blown into molten iron. It helps to remove any impurities through oxidation reactions.

Welders use oxygen to weld or cut metal. When fuel is burned in the presence of pure oxygen, the temperature of its flame is increased.

THE PERIODIC TABLE

All the elements are organized into a chart called the periodic table. It groups together elements with similar properties. Each square gives information about a particular element.

A Good Idea!

The periodic table was developed in the 1860s by a Russian chemist named Dmitri Mendeleev. He left gaps that were later filled in with new elements, as they were discovered.

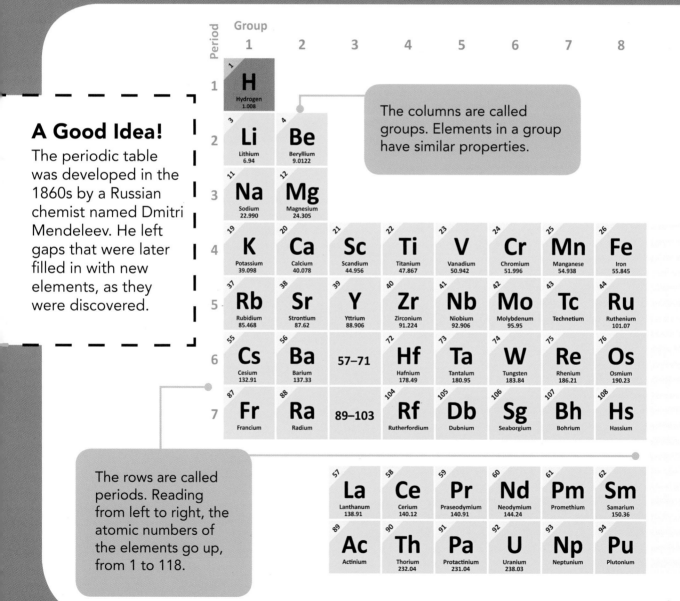

The columns are called groups. Elements in a group have similar properties.

The rows are called periods. Reading from left to right, the atomic numbers of the elements go up, from 1 to 118.

Every element has an atomic number. It shows how many protons are in each of its atoms. Oxygen's atomic number is 8.

The chemical symbol is one or two letters, often an abbreviation of the element's name. It is the same in all languages.

8

O

Oxygen
15.999

Each square shows the element's name. Different languages use different names.

A number shows the element's atomic weight. It is an average of the number of protons and neutrons in the different isotopes of an element.

9	10	11	12	13	14	15	16	17	18

Metalloids (semimetals)

Non–metals

Metals

									2 He Helium 4.0026
				5 B Boron 10.81	**6** C Carbon 12.011	**7** N Nitrogen 14.007	**8** O Oxygen 15.999	**9** F Fluorine 18.998	**10** Ne Neon 20.180
				13 Al Aluminum 26.982	**14** Si Silicon 28.085	**15** P Phosphorus 30.974	**16** S Sulfur 32.06	**17** Cl Chlorine 35.45	**18** Ar Argon 39.948
27 Co Cobalt 58.933	**28** Ni Nickel 58.693	**29** Cu Copper 63.546	**30** Zn Zinc 65.38	**31** Ga Gallium 69.723	**32** Ge Germanium 72.630	**33** As Arsenic 74.922	**34** Se Selenium 78.971	**35** Br Bromine 79.904	**36** Kr Krypton 83.798
45 Rh Rhodium 102.91	**46** Pd Palladium 106.42	**47** Ag Silver 107.87	**48** Cd Cadmium 112.41	**49** In Indium 114.82	**50** Sn Tin 118.71	**51** Sb Antimony 121.76	**52** Te Tellurium 127.60	**53** I Iodine 126.90	**54** Xe Xenon 131.29
77 Ir Iridium 192.22	**78** Pt Platinum 195.08	**79** Au Gold 196.97	**80** Hg Mercury 200.59	**81** Tl Thallium 204.38	**82** Pb Lead 207.2	**83** Bi Bismuth 208.98	**84** Po Polonium	**85** At Astatine	**86** Rn Radon
109 Mt Meitnerium	**110** Ds Darmstadtium	**111** Rg Roentgenium	**112** Cn Copernicium	**113** Nh Nihonium	**114** Fl Flerovium	**115** Mc Moscovium	**116** Lv Livermorium	**117** Ts Tennessine	**118** Og Oganesson

63 Eu Europium 151.96	**64** Gd Gadolinium 157.25	**65** Tb Terbium 158.93	**66** Dy Dysprosium 162.50	**67** Ho Holmium 164.93	**68** Er Erbium 167.26	**69** Tm Thulium 168.93	**70** Yb Ytterbium 173.05	**71** Lu Lutetium 174.97

Lanthanide elements

95 Am Americium	**96** Cm Curium	**97** Bk Berkelium	**98** Cf Californium	**99** Es Einsteinium	**100** Fm Fermium	**101** Md Mendelevium	**102** No Nobelium	**103** Lr Lawrencium

Actinide elements

QUIZ

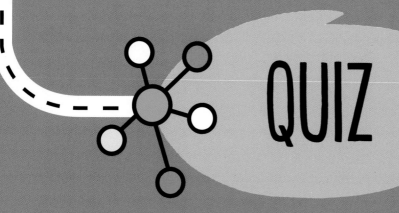

Try this quiz and test your knowledge of oxygen and elements! The answers are on page 32.

1

What are elements made of?

a. cells
b. atoms
c. cheese

2

What is ozone?

a. a compound of oxygen and zinc
b. an area of cold water in a swimming pool that makes you say "oh!"
c. an allotrope of oxygen with three atoms

3

What do you get when you combine iron and oxygen?

a. rust
b. diamond
c. a headache

4

How much of your body is made up of oxygen?

a. about 65 percent
b. it depends on how thirsty you are
c. just the sweat, blood, and urine

5

What do you call living things that don't need oxygen?

a. fish
b. anaerobes
c. just plain weird

6

Which two things are needed for respiration?

a. lungs and kidneys
b. a strong beat and a catchy tune
c. glucose and oxygen

7

What is the scientific name for burning?

a. combustion
b. compression
c. confusion

8

Why do mountain climbers sometimes carry oxygen tanks?

a. to melt snow at the mountaintop
b. to breathe when the high-altitude air is too thin
c. it makes them look like real professionals

GLOSSARY

allotropes different forms of the same element. Their atoms are arranged in different patterns.

anaerobe living thing that can release energy without needing oxygen

atmosphere the layers of gases that surround the earth

atom the smallest possible unit of a chemical element

bond to form a link with atoms of the same element or of a different element

carbohydrates compounds such as sugars and starches, which are made from carbon, hydrogen, and oxygen

carbon dioxide gas found in the air that plants need to survive

cell the smallest unit of life. All plants and animals are made of cells.

chemical change when one substance reacts with another to form a new substance

chemical property something that is observed during or after a chemical reaction

combustion chemical reaction of oxygen and a fuel, which releases heat and light

compound substance made of two or more different elements bonded together

condense change from a gas to a liquid

crust the hard, outermost layer of Earth

electron a tiny particle of an atom with a negative charge

element a substance that cannot be broken down or separated into other substances

energy the ability to do work. Energy can take many different forms.

fuel anything that can be burned as a source of energy, such as wood or gasoline

gas matter that is neither liquid or solid

hydrocarbons compounds made up of carbon and hydrogen atoms, which occur in oil, coal, and gas

isotopes different forms of the same element. Isotopes of an element have different numbers of neutrons.

liquid matter that is neither solid nor gas

mass the total amount of matter in an object or space

molecule the smallest unit of a substance that has all the properties of that substance. Molecules are made up of atoms.

neutron a particle in the nucleus of an atom with no electrical charge

nucleus the center of an atom

oxidation reaction chemical reaction in which oxygen bonds to another element to form a new substance

ozone allotrope of oxygen that has molecules made up of three oxygen atoms

photosynthesis the process by which a plant uses sunlight to change water and carbon dioxide into food

physical property a property that that can be observed without changing the material

proton a positively charged particle in the nucleus of an atom

react to undergo a chemical change when combined with another substance

respiration chemical process in which cells break down substances in order to release energy

FURTHER RESOURCES

BOOKS

Arbuthnott, Gill. *Your Guide to the Periodic Table.* New York, NY: Crabtree Publishing Company, 2016.

Callery, Sean, and Miranda Smith. *Periodic Table.* New York, NY: Scholastic Nonfiction, 2017.

Hurt, Avery Elizabeth. *Oxygen.* New York, NY: Enslow Publishing, 2019.

LaPlante, Walter. *What Makes Fire Burn?* New York, NY: Gareth Stevens, 2016.

Mason, Paul. *Your Breathtaking Lungs and Rocking Respiratory System.* New York, NY: Crabtree Publishing Company, 2016.

Stewart, Melissa. *Water.* Washington, DC: National Geographic, 2014.

WEBSITES

Go here for amazing facts about oxygen: **www.ducksters.com/science/chemistry/oxygen.php**

This website has facts about ozone and up-to-date images of the ozone hole: **ozonewatch.gsfc.nasa.gov**

Learn about all the elements using this interactive periodic table: **www.rsc.org/periodic-table/**

Learn more about combustion and how it works: **science.howstuffworks.com/environmental/earth/geophysics/fire1.htm**

INDEX

Quiz answers
1. b; 2. c; 3. a; 4. a; 5. b;
6. c; 7. a; 8. b